THE WAY HOME

Reflections on American Beauty

Jeffrey Bilhuber
THE WAY HOME
Reflections on American Beauty

Photography by William Abranowicz

RIZZOLI
NEW YORK

New York · Paris · London · Milan

CONTENTS

INTRODUCTION

Every day we find ways to share the ongoing stories of our lives with families and friends. Words, whether written or spoken, help us tell our tales. So does music, and especially song. Illustrations, be they photographs, watercolors, drawings, or paintings, are another way to communicate what we want to say, record, and remember. The furniture, art, architecture, and decoration, the trappings that we gather and arrange in the rooms we inhabit, also speak, whether mutely or assertively. Our homes are central to the narratives of self that we construct and pass on to our children, our families, our friends, and loved ones, and to the generations that follow all of us. Those in this book both reflect and are part of my own evolution. They represent for me a rather Arcadian ideal, and a specifically American one at that. This ideal is witness to the times that surround us, and how we choose to record it.

The projects I've cherished most these past few years, and the projects I'm presenting here, are those that I feel speak volumes about the people who live in them: they reveal home truths rather than, like so many American interiors, constructing domestic fictions about desired lifestyles. These interiors evoke personality, emotion, and mood. They conjure atmosphere, but don't pontificate about style. They express sensibility and character, without belaboring status or class. They are as different from one another as we human beings, yet they have in common a certain type of backdrop that embraces wildly disparate elements: Georgian sideboards, japanned corner cupboards, ebonized armchairs, wicker sofas,

Indian ikats, or painted cottage dressers. With a uniquely American beauty that only our national heritage offers, these rooms happily reconcile high and low, rare and common, handsome and homely from across the spectrum of cultures and periods. These kinds of interiors, democratic as they are, reveal the power of decoration to do more than preconceive a future or prestidigitate a past.

Rooms can, and often do, reveal intimate stories of lives lived in a specific time and place, because decoration of a certain kind embodies the unique capacity to tell the truth. Houses may do the same, just on a more epic scale. When they do, they demonstrate decoration at its most artful and enlightened. That occurs very rarely, and only when there is trust. When a decorator is offered the opportunity to put his ear to one's heart, he can create rooms that breathe the same essence as those who will live in them.

Growth is an evolutionary process. History is too. As we mature, we gain insight into our interior lives as well as our physical ones. Most of us require time to find our way to the houses we're meant to inhabit, places that seem to fit us only over time, and become better with each passing milestone or year. As a decorator I prefer when people come to me with a few or more touchstones that matter to them, that are part of their personal histories, simply because decoration is a dialogue between person and place.

I am uneasy with a clean slate. When my clients come to me with furniture, or art, or mementos that they love, I breathe a sigh of relief. Objects that are close to a person or family obviously present me with insights into individual taste and preferences. They reveal far more than mere taste. When objects have meaning—and those that we keep usually do—they are repositories of emotion, memories made manifest. If we love these objects, if they embody our connections to family, to aspects of our personal history, to special events or places, they become evidence of good lives moving forward, the hallmarks of arrival, and the path we've taken to reach home. Some things we love without explanation or question, simply because they've always been with us, regardless of whether their intrinsic value has anything to do with their extrinsic appearance. Others have an allure that develops as we covet and finally purchase them, when they, in turn, become our pride and joy.

Increasingly, I find myself drawn to images of a certain kind of domestic bliss from other distant times. Even though I have no interest in slavishly recreating the appointments of eighteenth-, nineteenth-, or even early twentieth-century residences, their comforts seem very appropriate to the spirit with which we live today. They provide flashpoints, moments of illumination and invention—the sort of inspiration that I then filter into the contemporary environment I'm creating for the here and now. That, to me, is what great modern decorating should be. That's what the houses in this book represent. However directly or indirectly influenced by history they may be—and some are more so than others—they feel modern because they

respond to the times we live in. They're building their foundations from history and memory, conjuring up a mood or a spirit that comforts with the familiar and previously experienced. They nurture these connections to our past, encouraging it to sustain us in a kind of emotional wave. Far more than assemblages of singular objects, these rooms are filled with the stories and reflections of their inhabitants. Their atmosphere and moodiness inform us about what gives their owners comfort and pleasure. They embody what I think of as a uniquely American perspective, and a distinctively American way of living. In many ways they reflect a certain contentment, and, I hope, to some growing degree, a few proven and rather old-fashioned values.

Context is essential to all great decoration. In many cases, it dictates our choices. Americans understand that it is their obligation and right to sample many decorative and cultural traditions— our own, and others. We prize ease and comfort in our domestic lives. We're very confident. We look to our future optimistically, and to our past with an understanding and empathy that only a new country can achieve. We are less hidebound, less rigorous than other cultures that embrace order and formality. American rooms are American precisely because they endow us with the liberty to be comfortable and enlightened: they are rooms where good things are put to their proper use and where not-so-good things remain to remind us that there's great joy and individuality to be found in the informal and less-than-perfect. We enthusiastically embrace and encourage appropriating bits and pieces from other cultures and across history, because we Americans are curious. We explore all worlds. Then we make choices that are uniquely our own, putting our stamp, our fingerprints, on these objects as we combine them.

Our rooms and houses contain the story of our evolving lives. They provide us with a narrative of our maturation, of how we've grown, and of how most of us continue to revisit, in one way or another, certain memories and the objects that have defined them.

Anyone can live beautifully and comfortably if they want to, if it matters to them. I don't believe that it's possible for any of us to do it all. Each of us needs help. We all benefit from the guidance of those people we trust and love.

As I decorator I do two things particularly well: I listen, and I make creative decisions. One is essential to the other. I have always found the most compelling and attractive rooms clearly reflect the individual—or the family—at home. These rooms, these houses, and homes, tell public stories of private lives. They are the tales I have chosen to tell here. I am interested far less in the individual objects or their materials than in the atmosphere of a place and its distinctive spirit, its specific approach to how we nest and the comforts that we find within our four, or occasionally more, walls. The interiors in this book are personal worlds, inward facing, and autobiographical about the people and the daily lives of those who inhabit them. They are

reflections of personal histories and family life, not grand gestures of presentation. They contain a sort of existence I would like to discover behind any closed door: replete with great pleasures and comforts, all of which play a role in informing us about who we are as we travel somewhat introspectively, listening, sensing, hearing our hearts beat, and finding our essential selves.

When everything at home contributes to the story of the house and of those who live there, that place—be it house, home, or heart—cannot be anywhere else than where it is. In places like these, it's possible to understand the spirit and the rhythms of the lives lived within, day after day, because their presence is visible and palpable. In houses like these, there's always someone home.

TAKING THE LONG WAY HOME

The admirable pursuit of a curiously timeless aesthetic

Jenny and Trey Laird are a quintessential New York story. They were college sweethearts at the University of Texas, and in many ways, they still are. Originally from Nacogdoches, the oldest town in Texas, Trey has built his advertising and branding company, Laird+Partners, into an international powerhouse. Jenny grew up in a family that embraced the pleasure of creative expression and gloried in celebrating the domestic narrative. She talks fondly about her mother's and her grandmother's houses and how they exist in her mind in a very specific place and time. Jenny has told me tales of visits to her grandmother's house and a certain fox fur piece, complete with glass eyes, she inevitably discovered curled up in a different location every time she arrived. Her always-tinkering grandmother had found dozens of spots where this fox looked "absolutely perfect!"—tucked into a bookcase, wrapped around a lamp, peeking through the balusters of a staircase. I find it equally remarkable that a very young Jenny noticed these deft moves and delighted in the sensibility behind them.

PRECEDING PAGES: *Carved into the marble mantel is a heraldic ornament, typical of this period in New York.* LEFT: *A lacquered hibachi doubles as a cachepot.* OPPOSITE: *The center medallion of an antique suzani reiterates the shape of the sofa.*

12

Both of the Lairds are devout in their reverence for the creative process. Every day Trey departs for work, where he immerses himself in a very similar vocabulary: whether creating a campaign for Tory Burch or Tommy Hilfiger, he conjures a visual storyboard that aids in delivering a message. Jenny and Trey carry on highly animated conversations about color, form, pattern, and texture; their loves, likes, and dislikes are part of the fabric of their days, and have been since the two of them met. They know how to distill the essence of these discussions and communicate it to those who are receptive.

Their house—a discreet town house near Carl Schurz Park and Gracie Mansion—is in a hushed and seductive neighborhood that feels one step removed from the hubbub of the city, a place where

you can still find a row of mews houses or glory in a bower of wisteria draping an entrance door. In this small corner of the city, there are clapboard houses with porches and Queen Anne style buildings of powerful red brick. When they purchased it fifteen years ago, they knew well that it would be years before they could do any significant work so they artfully built their possessions—a chair here, a candlestick there, a drawing, a carpet—successfully creating a certain bohemian sophisticate atmosphere. After we finished their village house in Bridgehampton (see pp. 180–97), they could no longer push off the inevitable renovation of their house in town. They now had the time and ability to tinker with the structure and to create the rooms they'd anticipated for so very long.

We started with the idea that it was going to be a rather streamlined and edited house—late midcentury modern—with an '80s-style jet-set clarity, verging on monochromatic. Through a year of creative evolution, really confident colors started to enter our discussions. There were invigorating bursts of deep claret, saturated Persian blue, and intense chromium yellow. Recently, talks of emerald green have also begun to enter the picture. From there, we began taking small steps toward something more unusual and evocative. As their collection of antique carpets has grown, the house has taken on an even more bohemian splendor that continues to develop in an almost nineteenth-century way.

When they told me that they were going to pave the entire ground floor of the house—entry, kitchen, and breakfast room—in an interlocking, black-glazed Moroccan tile, I was enchanted. I have seen Moroccan tiles in nearly every color, but never black. It's a decision that defines them

LEFT AND OPPOSITE: *A meticulous still life on a japanned cabinet includes an ivory candlestick and a nineteenth-century English watercolor.* OVERLEAF: *A woven silk ikat in an unusual fish-scale pattern covers his and her reading chairs in the breakfast room.*

If you live in a New York City town house, you lead a fairly transparent existence because the street-facing windows offer passersby illuminating glimpses behind the facade. When Trey asked to place the same fabric—a charming and flowery printed cotton—in all of the windows on the street, I thought it a brilliant solution because it harmonized the entire facade.

At the foundation of all the rooms are troweled-plaster and resin-striated walls—a very good backdrop, humble, settled, and malleable, becoming anything that you want them to be, the perfect foil for the story inserted upon them. Typical of the period with their radius-form openings, all of the fireplace mantels are original to the house. Many New Yorkers are so used to seeing these that we almost take them for granted. It was reassuring to find that these had been preserved. On the primary floor, Jenny and Trey removed the partition wall that usually separates the front from the rear parlors, and inserted French doors—a more European idea, which makes you aware of the rooms that follow each other. I gave a similar sensibility to the placement of the living room furniture: it occupies all of the room rather than just the perimeter, and turns to address the center rather than ignore it. It also happens to cut right in front of those glass paned doors, as if they're simply not there.

perfectly. That floor, once seen, builds a sense of anticipation for the experiences that will follow. Once installed, the floor surprised everyone by behaving like a drum, echoing and amplifying every sound. You couldn't slice bread without covering your ears. If someone would say, "What an attractive room," the response would invariably be "What? It's a tomb?" "No, it's an attractive room," followed by a reply of "You want a drink so soon?" Needless to say, and by mutual agreement, we all conceded to a ravishingly threadbare animal-spot carpet that descended upon the house like a blanket on a baby.

LEFT: *A gilded Swedish Art Deco bracketed clock hangs on the kitchen's tiled walls.* OPPOSITE: *The breakfast room opens to a trellised garden in the spirit of Elsie de Wolfe.* OVERLEAF, LEFT: *The living room, looking toward the library.* OVERLEAF, RIGHT: *Neutral walls frame intervals of intense color.*

most ethereal lightweight linen we could find, because Trey was willing to concede to Jenny's long-held desire for bed hangings only if they were void of any decoration or embellishment—a handkerchief of sorts. They are a triumph! The lamps on the outside of these curtains are lined in pink dupioni silk, a concept so fussy that Trey simply didn't want to get it. Jenny did. She won him over—as well she should have. This design dialogue, like so many others, continues to this day.

After all the changes we've made to this house, it still retains the hallmarks of their personalities; in fact, it amplifies them. Everything that was here before remains, yet the house itself has become more receptive to what gives them pleasure. One of the plentiful joys of knowing them is visiting after a three- or four-week hiatus and realizing that some objects may have found new locations. Some have simply found the right place after all, while others will always be in transit. Jenny and Trey view the world with an editor's eye, so they're constantly scripting their domestic landscape like the great art directors they are—and the audience they will become.

Jenny and Trey are meticulous about their books, which are all well-read, well-loved, and meticulously arranged in the library. It's Negoro-lacquered walls lie in deep shadow on the other side of the French doors. Clearly there's an aura of the exotic here, a mystery that you accept without attempting to solve. I adore a room in deep shadow.

Jenny, true to form, drove the decisions in the bedroom—a pale gray-and-white cloud at the top of the house. She wanted a place to quietly retreat or retire to. There has been much talk recently of a very old-fashioned shop she's discovered in Palm Beach that sells only bed jackets, a new and consuming 'must-have' that I highly endorse, if only for the look of this very pretty room. The bed hangings are the simplest,

Old-fashioned African violets sit on the living room's center table. The walls are covered in a combination of combed plaster and resin. The chromium yellow ceramic vessel anchors the airy room's velvet-skirted table.

LEFT: *An ink on paper work by Tim Rollins + K.O.S. contributes to the still life on the mantel.* OPPOSITE: *One of a pair of Jansen lacquered tables.* OVERLEAF, LEFT: *A rare late-eighteenth-century Persian silk velvet ikat panel unfurls over the banquette.* OVERLEAF, RIGHT: *The library directly overlooks the garden.*

ABOVE: *Looking from the library through the French doors to the living room.*
OPPOSITE: *Covering the library sofa is an African-style printed cotton in burnished gold and white. The 1966 screen print,* Jackie II, *is by Andy Warhol.*

LEFT: *One of a pair of bronze lacquered gueridons by Laurence Montano.* OPPOSITE: *The sculpture mounted to the lacquered wall is* Silver River—Mississippi *by Maya Lin.* OVERLEAF, LEFT: *An American papier-mâché chair inlaid with abalone captures diffused light in the master bedroom.* OVERLEAF, RIGHT: *The tufted reading chair was originally designed by Mark Hampton for his daughter Kate.*

CALEIGH AND AVA
A chair near the window

Most people think a house must be vast to be seductive for a decorator. That is simply not true, and, many times, contrary to what I believe. When someone who loves what I do calls, I listen. When that person is palpably in love with decoration, art, antiques, comfort, and color, I'm even more than intrigued. This family piles high their books on decoration, design, and architecture, and their joy in domestic beauty is boundless. When they called, they had recently moved with two young girls from their longtime Manhattan apartment to a beautifully crafted, properly proportioned cottage, set on an idyllic Connecticut lane overarched by gloriously mature trees. They placed their absolute trust in me, certain that remarkable results would follow, allowing me to do what I do best—make creative decisions.

Carrie Wallack is at ease with color, exuberant, and fearless. But to adore color and pattern both? To delight in giant floral bouquets sidling up gleefully to great candy-cane stripes? Could this really be? I actually found myself putting on the brakes just to be certain that Russell, her husband, was equally enthusiastic about all of this. I'd not met him, which made me just this side of nervous. She reassured me not to detour and that her direction was a collective thought. I'm a very old-fashioned guy, and these rooms, despite their exuberance and the full-on profusion of color and pattern, feel very traditional—what I refer to as 'tradition with horsepower.'

Because the house doesn't have a visible or actively used back door, one is compelled to use the front, which they do, all day, every day, all year long. In a nod to the great American decorating firm Parish-Hadley, I painted and grained the chevron floor pattern in the entry hall. Then I added the Gustavian painted drop-front desk, which they've filled with lovely photographs of their children, Caleigh and Ava, and their friends' children—so much more appropriate here than the usual hall table. Certainly it's the friendly, neighborly gesture—and absolutely fitting in a neighborhood as close as this one.

Prepared simply to write the living room off as impossibly small, and therefore beyond rescue, Carrie was convinced that there might be nothing I could do to save it. That's all I needed to rise to the occasion. I worked enthusiastically to reassure her that this 'too-small' room had all the qualities any larger quarters could ever have. It needed to feel to them as if, after a move from the 'big house,' they were happily settled into a cottage, beloved trappings and touchstones intact. My first gambit was a vast sofa to push the room's boundaries. Called an Aiken's sofa, hailing from North Carolina and built for languid afternoons on big porches, it's a humble wood-framed form that is luxurious in scale, if not material. The brownness of the other furniture—the Jacobean oak chest, for instance—grounds the room, giving it deep roots. Alongside a painted French balloon-back chair, that chest represents a kind of

PRECEDING PAGES: *John Singer Sargent's influence on this portrait of the children is an appropriate touch for the character of these rooms.* OPPOSITE: *A detail of the charming, memento-filled living room mantel.* ABOVE: *At Caleigh's request, her bedroom is painted plum. The lamp is a converted French seltzer bottle.*

kitchen furniture—just the way your auntie would with the leftover can of paint from the trim and molding. Then I pushed the tufted chair and a lovely old rattan ottoman into the corner by the street-facing windows, because these windows have a sort of gravitational pull, in addition to rather splendid proportions. The children play there much of the day and watch the neighbors walk their dogs or wave to their friends. The delightful Mrs. Wallack found this to be so inconceivable, and yet so very tempting that, when the girls are in school and she's finished her chores, she sits there sipping tea, nibbling a few contraband cookies, and peeking past the café curtains too!

With all those gorgeous English Sheraton chairs in the dining room, we obviously didn't need more in the breakfast room. The large settee does the job perfectly. It may be a tad difficult to get in and out of, but they wouldn't move it for the world. It's become Carrie's favorite place to settle in the morning, just as the tufted, floral linen chair is for her in the afternoon.

personal history to me: the pieces may not obviously belong together, but they certainly could have shared a collective past in an earlier house, and perhaps even another house before that.

For years I've been honing strategies for making dining rooms in small houses behave in a casual and modern fashion: you simply can't drop a table into the middle of the room and call it finished. The Wallacks' became this wondrous little furnished sitting room that happened to have a table—the one from their New York apartment. Of polished fruitwood and oddly too urban a shape for its new surroundings, I painted it to match the room—like

ABOVE AND OPPOSITE: *A pair of stylish 1930s French fauteuils in the living room. The sconces are electrified English coaching lanterns. An Edward Burne-Jones painting from the collection of Ambassador Vernon Reed presides rather grandly over the room.* OVERLEAF: *Soft, box-pleated valances in the English fashion dress the handsomely scaled street-facing windows.*

PRECEDING PAGES: *Many of the drawings, paintings, and watercolors are American botanicals.* LEFT: *The owners' vintage children's books in a hanging corner cabinet.* OPPOSITE: *In the dining room, a set of six English William IV chairs are covered in apple green leather with contrasting, watermelon-colored welting and trim.*

One day I arrived to find a woven willow basket filled with the little birds that you see on the mantel, or floating on the bookcases, or nesting on the japanned corner cupboard. They had belonged to Carrie's mother-in-law, who was an artist (her work pops up in all these rooms) and clearly a very creative woman. I love mementos you can squirrel away, and I dug straight into that basket of birds to find their new perches. They add an enormous charm that no amount of furniture we might purchase could ever replicate.

The watercolors, drawings, paintings, and nineteenth-century American still lifes are lovely found bits, lending an air of enchantment next to all the other family art and heirlooms. When I returned to this house to start taking photographs, the glorious painting by Edward Burne-Jones had appeared over the living room mantel. Purchased after the house was finished, it is academic perfection. The painting came from the distinguished collection of Ambassador Vernon Reed, a man of refined taste and good manners whom I have admired for decades. It proves that the house now does what it was meant to do and that it has become a catalyst for the Wallacks, just as it was for me.

I think that everyone except me was a bit terrified of how I was going to pull together the family room, but it became as spontaneous a thought and creative a solution as all the other rooms that we labored over. The pair of orange damask patterned chairs represent a nod to a mythical earlier house that could have been theirs— rather like the Indian screen, which our decorative painter, Phil Bland, worked over until this lovely light finish emerged. It's a softer patina that removed any hint of a tourist component. It's all rather charming now, I must say. The room is a triumph, lived in and well-loved!

ABOVE: *A gilded and lacquered stand near the entry hall.* OPPOSITE: *A charming and robust primitive painting of a three-masted brigantine in the dining room.* OVERLEAF, LEFT: *An American schoolhouse chalkboard in the dining room features the day's menu.* OVERLEAF, RIGHT: *On the breakfast room table, an enchanting collection of English Staffordshire ware from the brilliant antiques dealer John Rosselli.*

LEFT AND OPPOSITE: *A pair of Italian painted bookcases has chicken wire doors.* OVERLEAF, LEFT: *The profusion of colors and patterns is spontaneous and uninhibited.* OVERLEAF, RIGHT: *The bedside lamps are very blurry and saturated Chinese blue-and-white glazed ceramics with pink card shades.*

FIRST LIGHT
East of the Sun (West of the Moon)

When I conjure the emotional content of a house, I begin with the familiar, with memory and dreams, often intertwined. It might be a lasting but vague recollection, a comfort that lingers like the memory of a glorious rose garden, long past its peak. These clients had memories, dreams, and recollections in abundance. They had imagined a house in the dunes by the sea—a hippie house, they called it, with a bit of amusement and gravitas. They had an ideal in mind, like that perfect summer rental that you come across unexpectedly and is yours for only a season. That spoke to me of a yearning to recapture, idealistically and nostalgically, a utopian spirit of innocence—an endless 'summer of love.' This concept was charged with a certain intellectualism, a sort of overriding optimism and volcanic creativity that recalls a time when we were much more conscious of what we were saying than where we were seated when we said it.

This little house is that dream of a place. A timbered seaside cottage, buried in the sand—profoundly poetic, with wooden planked walls the colors of driftwood and oyster shells that speak of vanished days. Those walls had been painted, and painted again. Uninterrupted vistas of the sea, sky,

PRECEDING PAGES: *The eastern edge of Nantucket is well known for fog-bound mornings.* LEFT: *An elaborately carved Jiangsu Chinese lantern in the stair hall.* OPPOSITE: *A serpent-footed English garden bench at the side entry.* OVERLEAF, LEFT: *Lichen on split cedar rails.* OVERLEAF, RIGHT: *The boardwalk traverses rosehips and spartina.*

58

and shore make this place utterly alluring, but what I love is its relation to the open night skies and endless dunes of sand. Set back deeply from the tide line, it nestles into a tidal pool that flows into a preserve ten feet away from the back porch. A white oak boardwalk, remainders of the barn flooring used throughout the cottage, winds from the house to the water's edge. There's a wonderful ceremony that comes with that serpentine promenade to the sea, through the sand and land that connects you to it. All of that contributes to the atmosphere of this house far more than if it were planted at ocean's edge. You'd be as happy here on a stormy winter's day as you are on a clear July morning.

East of the sun and west of the moon
We'll build a dream house of love,
Close to the sun in the day
Near to the moon at night
We'll live in a lovely way, dear
Sharing our love in the pale moonlight

Just you and I, forever and a day
Love will not die; we'll keep it that way
Up among the stars we'll find a harmony of life
to a lovely tune
East of the sun and west of the moon, dear
East of the sun and west of the moon

This is a love story that embraces its surroundings emotionally and physically, as it does the family that lives here. That spirit infuses everything in it and all the decisions we made during the process of its creation. Part of the delight comes naturally from surroundings

that are filled with the comforts of the familiar, including those objects, books, and furniture that occasion happy or tender memories, either recent or from many seasons and summers ago.

So much of the furniture and so many objects in this house come from the owners' previous houses, or from their parents' houses. Her mom stitched all the glorious needlepoint cushions that we flung about the family room, a skillfully converted winter garage, as well as the bellpulls, footstool covers, and pillows that pop up everywhere else in the house. Nicknamed the 'terrine queen,' her mother had also assembled a trove of those tabletop treasures—a lifetime of curiosities and memories, really—which we sorted through to

LEFT: *The needlepoint bell pull at the front door is a treasured family heirloom.* OPPOSITE: *The floor of the family room and winter garage is white-painted brick. The sleeping loft is accessible by ladder only. Masses of needlepoint pillows dot the upholstery.*

through a beaded door is a wonderful feeling, a tactile thrill—you have to touch it, it brushes softly against you, you can hear it, an amazing sensory perception. Yet it's simply wooden beads strung together and bought in the local gift store, a place appropriately named 'The Sunken Ship.'

The owners usually arrive in early spring when the first flowers are up, so as not to miss the celebration of Daffodil Weekend. They go long-board surfing. They go deep-sea fishing. They bike everywhere and play board games on the floor on rainy days. The fireplaces are well used, and the house has the scent of salt and smoke. There's a sort of harmony to all of these elements, a certain confirmation of their expectedness. In reverie and in reality, this house couldn't be anything other than it is—and although other houses built close to the tide may wash away in a storm, this house will remain. Some houses never get loved or lived in as this one is. I honestly think that there's every reason to suppose that this house could have taken 250 years to produce. Yet if it had, we wouldn't have been able to enjoy it. And yes, perhaps it would have been an even better dream if they'd simply walked into a place that already existed and said, 'Perfect, we'll take it.' But if they had, then it wouldn't be their house at all.

use here. As we opened box after box, I fell in love with every one, whether it was pewter or blue-and-white transfer ware or something that looked as if it would have been filled with conch chowder in the Bahamas. These rooms couldn't exist without such flourishes—the real, tangible, storytelling components from past lives. They are why I was able to cobble this all together to build the atmosphere of the place: eighteenth-century continental furniture cheek to jowl with midcentury finds, the profusion of needlepoint cushions next to hand-blocked linens near an Edwardian chair and a 1960s teakwood table.

The only real reference to that mythical hippie house is a doorway hung with beads. To walk

LEFT: *A fine-wale cotton corduroy covers the Rosekrantz armchair.*
OPPOSITE: *The converted winter garage serves as a catchall for pleasurable summer pursuits. The barn doors open onto bear grass and beach paths.*
OVERLEAF: *In the living room, a pair of English spoon-back chairs, an ebonized ratcheted wing chair, and a French chestnut garden table contribute to the room's expansive mix of periods and styles.*

OPPOSITE: *Summer flowers from Bartlett's Farm adorn the mantel.* RIGHT: *Among the treasures is an enchanting photo of Snoop Dogg, the family Chihuahua, an accidental show dog.* OVERLEAF, LEFT: *The dining table in the corner opens directly onto the living room.* OVERLEAF, RIGHT: *Part of the owners' cache of terrines.*

PRECEDING PAGES: *A lobster-patterned weave covers a pair of sofas and a chair in the second-floor sitting room.* LEFT AND OPPOSITE: *The room's white-painted plank walls are almost bare of ornament. At the foot of the sofa is a provincial French ottoman covered in needlepoint.* PAGE 76: *A view into the family office, past a beaded doorway.* PAGE 77: *A flat-weave cotton dhurrie in a bargello flame-stitch pattern covers the floor of the master bedroom.* PAGE 78: *The path to the beach.* PAGE 79: *A porch swing hangs at the back of the house.*

AN UNFINISHED HISTORY

Bearing witness to our past and present

I remember, not long after I arrived in New York, seeing blocks of contiguous brownstones, Manhattan's most iconic and pervasive late-nineteenth-century architectural vernacular. There were avenues and streets of them, precursors to the city's enlightened twentieth-century expression. We've lost so many of them whole, or in part, including the rather ceremonial front stairs and stoop. I'm puzzled as to where all those cast-iron balustrades went. They just vanished. Gone.

This particular brownstone sits on a block of such old-world perfection that it's quintessentially cinematic, in a Nora Ephron sort of way. During the years it hid under wraps, I found myself walking by regularly. I've always been drawn to this particular stretch of low-profile houses and I happen to have the good fortune of living just a few doors away. Without fanfare, the scaffolding came down. I watched as one van, then two, then three arrived and departed one after the other. Move-in day! I did what neighbors should do: I brought them an apple pie. Well, not really an apple pie, but something much more delicious—a *tarte tatin*, composed of apples cooked in a saucepan and then inverted onto a caramelized crust. A true favorite of mine.

PRECEDING PAGES: *A quintessential Upper East Side block lined in low-rising town houses, carriage houses, stables, and apartment buildings.* LEFT: *The restored brownstone facade.*

I discovered that, like so many New Yorkers, the young couple of the house were transplants—originally from the Northwest, a part of this country I love for the 'no-nonsense' people it produces. I also learned that their house, now so appropriately restored by Peter Pennoyer, had been more of an adventurous obstacle course than they had initially expected. Stoutly they carried on, but with a bit less enthusiasm. Their finished house was splendid, just beginning to be furnished with their finds and discoveries, and one had the sense that their hopes were also being beautifully realized. Yet they felt that somehow the house needed to recover its spirit, as did they. This is when I, and that 'pie' arrived.

The restoration had infused the house's reclaimed rooms with the perfume of their original intent. Their remarkable beauty begins with the architecture, and all of my additional decorative elements built upon that. The rooms on the house's main reception floor—the piano nobile—were,

and now are, proper parlors in keeping with the original plan of the house, one of four brownstones designed by William McNamara in 1872 for the developer William McEvily.

As a decorator, nothing terrifies me more than starting with a clean slate, for how can one interpret personality in the absence of its expression? The slate was full here. A pair of true collectors, this couple makes decisions about the art and antiques they choose to live with only after assessing all their options in depth. Tellingly, a spectacular collection of eighteenth- and nineteenth-century Scottish and Irish furniture already existed, as did a burgeoning collection of paintings from the late twentieth and early twenty-first centuries, rather insightful touchstones. I started incorporating some

a traditional technique that creates a compelling atmospheric envelope with translucent, virtually tactile color. The rear parlor, a creamy crosshatched bas-relief, remains the largest and most formal of the receiving rooms—as it was meant to be. But it still needed to feel intimate for a rather large-scale room, so I designed a pair of fireside banquettes to offer up a gesture of embrace. Inherently more urbane and

twentieth-century pieces—lighting, in particular— to provide a little more connective tissue among the different periods. As I watched their contemporary artworks evolve these past few years, I realize they have made their way ever deeper into the world of art that is this city: befriending the artists whose works they collect, welcoming them into their house, celebrating them as friends or neighbors, creating community in the particular way that New Yorkers do.

Reflecting on historic houses of this period, one tends not to conjure rooms saturated in brilliant color. Yet vibrant color is historically accurate, and its addition activated the monochromatical backdrops I initially found here. The front parlor is a greyed-down pink—a variation of the brighter original that results from three different colors of glazing,

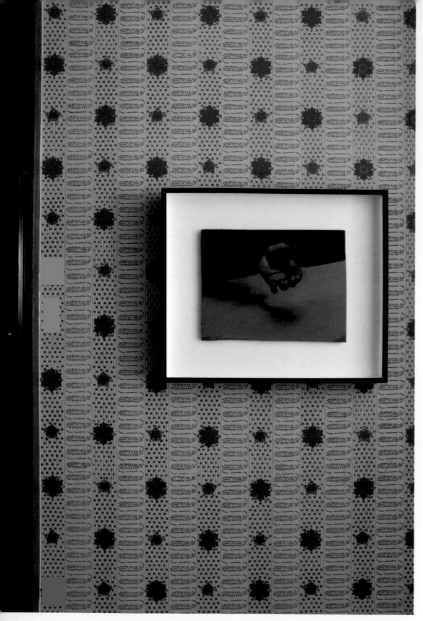

PRECEDING, LEFT: *The burnished marble mantle was designed by W. D. McLennan of Paisley, Scotland, who was known for designs that seemed to be Art Nouveau versions of Perpendicular Gothic.* PRECEDING, RIGHT: *A nineteenth-century English polychrome garden seat makes a charming side table.* LEFT AND OPPOSITE: *In the stair hall, art and antiques play an important role in defining the history of this house and its owners.*

simply cannot avoid Alex Katz's arresting oil on canvas, *5:30PM, Late May.* It demanded a darkened backdrop. Its astonishing green-based yellow fluorescence helped me understand the relationship of this room to the garden. An indigo-on-yellow cotton batik on the headchairs counterbalanced the painting's massive visual pull. Lining the curtains with that same yellow extended the painting's intensity in reverse, from the garden back into the room.

The two columns at the bottom of the staircase anchor the house. The sofa nestled between them acts as a seducer, something voluptuous to see from above, and a deeply comfortable vantage point to witness the cooking in an actively used kitchen. The mom of this house is a brilliant cook, an enthusiasm we share, and an even better baker, which I, alas, am not. Oh, how I wish I could bake a cake, a pie, a tarte!

This is a New York town house—an ever-changing part of an evolving city's historical fabric. Now it feels as if generations of the same family have always lived there, evolving in a rather natural way. It's a comfort to know your neighbors, to build on those friendships, and bear witness to a city that becomes your neighborhood.

formalized, with glorious carpets, the glint of gilding and crystal refractions, and a palette of softened color, this room has an appealingly ordered sensibility.

The center stair hall captivates all with a nineteenth-century documentary wallpaper that we had printed from the original blocks. The palette is so vivid and appropriate for the house's core—usually its darkest point. As a modern society we want to add light into dark spaces, but here I opted to solve the riddle rather differently: a strong sapphire-blue ground elevates the atmosphere of these interior depths by animating the space, enlivening rather than lightening.

My goals in the dining room were twofold. You

PAGES 92–95: *The owners'
late-nineteenth-century
Amritsar carpet unifies
a large formal sitting room.
A Joan Mitchell painting
presides over the sofa.* LEFT:
*One of two nineteenth-
century quillwork-decorated
rosewood and parcel-gilt
occasional tables.* OPPOSITE:
*The owners' meticulous
selection of materials,
trimmings, furniture,
and art gives the house a
deeply personal atmosphere.*

PRECEDING PAGES: *A work by Sigmar Polke hangs over the sitting room mantel.*
LEFT: *The molded plaster dentil detailing exemplifies the attention to historic precedent; the painting by Alex Katz moves it forward.*
OPPOSITE: *An amusing egg cup at the breakfast table.*

THINK OF ME WHEN FAR AWAY

Lives on sea and shore when distance brings us closer

I've always had a thing for Mary Beth, in her cloth-top Volkswagen with the 'WELUVMB' license plates. The truth is that just about everyone else does too. How could you not love a woman named Mary Beth? It's even sweeter when the name fits the frame. I don't think I've ever known another Mary Beth. I wish I had, or at least another like this. She is a radiant woman with a flawlessly pale complexion and glossy, raven-colored hair. She loves her husband, Chris, a very agreeable and handsome fellow, and she gets my trophy for 'World's Best Mom.'

Freshened by salty breezes billowing up from the sea, their house sits on a Nantucket high point, a beacon of light and clarity, and surprisingly transparent. When you enter this house, you see five complete rooms: the entrance hall you're standing in, the kitchen to the left, the living room to the right, the family room dead ahead, and, at the core, the open dining room with its scrubbed pedestal table. That large, central table pulls

PRECEDING PAGES: *In the family room, gingham camouflages the sofa's commodious proportions. Amethyst-colored, wave-patterned curtains billow in sea breezes rising above the bluff.* LEFT: *Vintage Fiestaware stacked in the glass-fronted pantry.*

*A shed roof protects the
guest cottage entry, set within
a pastoral greensward.*

everyone in; it's the anchor for the house's cruciform plan, the real and metaphorical heart of the family vortex. Mary Beth keeps a steady supply of sunflowers on that table throughout the summer, which speaks volumes about her outlook. I often think of her optimism, and when I dream of a house, it's this one I dream of.

To translate her effervescence into tangible form, I encouraged a palette of flatteringly pretty colors as clear, bright, and feminine as she is. That took a bit of hand-holding, but, because they were Mary Beth's hands, it was rather pleasant all around. In the living room, there's yellow the color of a lemon square and the same orange as an Orange Julius. Remember those? There's also the blue of an April sky and a green that foreshadows spring—restorative and reassuring.

Other than the curtains, I left this room free of pattern. The contrast infuses the room with a frisson of history's layers: the unexpected, isolated pattern gives the room its foundation, its past; the colors provide its future. Less than a generation ago, the sofa, curtains, and pillow fabrics would have matched. Now it appears as if Mary Beth and Chris have replaced the sofa fabric, faded after years in the sun, but not the curtains—and perhaps a beloved Labrador has dragged those coordinating pillows out to sea.

Shadow is perfection in any bedroom on a bright summer afternoon, so I always close the curtains in summer. That's what they're there for. The effect reminds me of the paintings by Walter

Gay, whose enchanting oils depict interiors with curtains drawn, an arc of light across a polished floor, refracted in faceted glass, animating the leaf of a plant, drawing our attention to a cool ring of water on the dresser, under a glass. The master bedroom contains a few wonderful 'Sailors' Valentines.' These sweet remembrances originated in nineteenth-century Barbados, a regular port of call for sailors far from home. There the local artisans crafted intricate shadow boxes with enchanting patterns on octagonal bases made of Cedrela (Spanish cedar) and frequently inscribed them with tender sentiments like 'Love the Giver,'

'Home Again,' or my favorite, 'Think of Me When Far Away.' They served as gifts for the sailors' woeful wives, sisters, and mothers. Remembrances, they marked the return, or impending return, of their loved ones.

Their library I intended as a sort of beacon to return home to—a lighthouse for the family. With a slightly tight and aptly named 'bay' window, the room faces the street that looks toward the sea. Shuttered windows encourage the whole family to congregate and watch television. The entire room—sofa, chairs, and walls—is as yellow as sunflowers, daffodils, and buttercups, so that passersby and family alike will take heart from it in the cool darkness of night.

With a living room, a ground-floor bedroom, and an upstairs bunk room, the guesthouse is a charming enclave unto itself. Canopy beds always win me over, especially when, like this one, they create their own airy rooms under high ceilings. Images of glorious Scandinavian bunkhouses—beds built into compartments, curtained for privacy—have tantalized me for years. I was so happy to realize the quartet of bunk beds we created here.

I know the shape of days past, present, and future in this house: sports, clambakes, and movies, often arranged by Mary Beth on the chalkboard. I am certain there will always be a sandy floor and a wet dog, teenagers in the pool and others coming from the beach, a cake in the oven and sunflowers on that handsome center table.

Mary Beth and Chris, with their children, live in Tokyo now and return to Nantucket for those long-awaited summers. I'm certain that this house is always close to their hearts, and like the Sailors' Valentines it contains, they think of it, beloved, when far, far away.

ABOVE: *A pair of intricately painted yellow glass hurricanes animates the tabletop.* OPPOSITE: *In the living room, an American Rococo console table is encrusted with oyster and abalone shells.* OVERLEAF: *Glimpsed through an internal window, the living room appears as a later addition, as if a porch had been converted.*

OPPOSITE: *A glass-sided, glass-topped display table contains a charming collection of beachcombing treasures.* RIGHT: *Two of four curtained bunks in the guest cottage.* OVERLEAF, LEFT: *A view down the long kitchen hall toward the coveted ground-floor guest room.* OVERLEAF, RIGHT: *A 1760 English walnut Queen Anne highboy adds a Yankee saltiness to the guest room.*

PRECEDING PAGES: *A pair of painted Arts and Crafts chairs in silhouette under the windows in the master bedroom.* LEFT: *Summer cosmos from the garden on a bedside table.* OPPOSITE: *A linen-draped canopy bed in the guest cottage offers temptation and comfort.*

DROPPING ANCHOR
Port Out, Starboard Home

I find that people come to decorators, and thus to home, in many ways. Sometimes it feels as if kismet is involved from the first meeting, thanks to an instantaneous sense of camaraderie. Other times you realize only later that the fine hand of destiny has been at work all along. With Andrew Drexel Allen, it was a bit of both. When he introduced himself so straightforwardly via e-mail to say that his SoHo loft could use my helping hand, I replied immediately and accepted the project within minutes of the initial conversation.

Soon after that fateful e-mail, I met Andrew downtown. There he stood, silhouetted in the half-light of an empty room in a triplex that was soon to become his own and that of his two sons. A handshake and a gentleman's agreement later, I got to work. Like many a devoted father, he wanted to provide a deeply comfortable, carefree house for his

boys when they came into the city for the weekends—a holiday spot, a getaway where they could be together as three 'men about town,' go googly-eyed at the nine-foot-tall leggy blonde models that appear to be everywhere in SoHo, be transfixed by the movies shooting around every corner, head uptown to the dinosaurs at the Museum of Natural History, or visit the Union Square Green Market for a fresh-from-the-farm treat.

I subsequently learned that Andrew serves as a director on the boards of two charitable foundations while on the board of trustees at Far Hills Country Day School and the Worldwide Orphans Foundation, and that his family has been in the wine business for nearly a century. His great-grandfather, Clarence Dillon, acquired a First Growth Bordeaux Chateau in 1935, and he and his family have nurtured those vineyards for four generations. That's when I realized that his devotion to family and tradition embraced those terms in their most expansive sense.

As I thought about what the rooms of his loft would look like with the children in them, I saw a family picnic—the guys playing games on the floor, relaxed and at ease, reading by the fireplace, or having lunch at the very long table. Because I knew it was a men's club, so to speak, I knew none of them would have patience for anything too 'done-up' or fancy. It was liberating,

PRECEDING PAGES: *Robert Mangold's* Two Columns A, *2004, an etching with relief on mulberry paper, hangs on white-washed walls.* OPPOSITE, FAR LEFT: *A pretty, hand-blocked linen graces a French bergère sitting near a portrait of the owner as a young boy.* OPPOSITE, BOTTOM: *A bolt of vintage outdoor fabric unfurls on the floor for picnics.* ABOVE: *The family's Bordeaux on the dining room table.* OVERLEAF: *A family portrait.*

LEFT: *A recent addition, the piano rests comfortably near the windows.* OPPOSITE: *Curtains hung from bamboo poles amplify the scale of a classic SoHo loft.* OVERLEAF: *Masses of fresh-cut eucalyptus from the Union Square Greenmarket act as an aromatic.*

actually, to come up with decoration that is at its heart utilitarian: good-looking but not overprocessed, overthought, or detail-obsessed. These rooms are so much fun to be in because they're so very well grounded. Assembling all the elements was one of those lovely experiences when decisiveness and discipline were completely in sync. I knew I needed a lot of furniture in a very short period of time, and I decided that I would only get what I loved, and none would be prohibitively expensive. Period. That may have added to the allure. Time was very much of the essence, so I selected furnishings based on comfort and practicality and what was readily available, knowing that all the pieces—the bamboo chairs, the commodious sofas, the glazed ceramic tables from the 1970s—would fit together in an

exceedingly appealing way. That haphazardness is what gives this place the feeling of a holiday house—of rooms put together spontaneously, but over time, as if they had evolved over the course of numerous summers, or as tenant after tenant moved the elements around to fit individual needs. Therein lies the joy.

If you look closely, you'll see that a palette of various reds underpins all the decorative decisions. Those reds came first, and I'm sure they have something to do with my idea of an industrial aesthetic—or at least an industrial loft in the SoHo of the 1960s, pure in its way and full of homesteading artists, not the SoHo of today, the burgeoning shopping paradise. Red is a color that takes the 'found' out of the found objects, transforming them into premeditated choices. So all of the light fixtures are red enamel. I think the hodgepodge of different styles looks as if Andrew has accumulated everything over time, adding another piece whenever he found it tempting.

PRECEDING, LEFT: *The living room dressed for a picnic.* PRECEDING, RIGHT: *Mother, a 1985 aquatint by Julian Schnabel, and a 1960s canvas,* White Field 1, *by Robert Rahway Zakanitch, dominate the north end of the loft.* OPPOSITE: *The boys' bedrooms are galleries for their artwork.* RIGHT: *A 1960s California School tree trunk table adds sculptural form to the mix.* PAGES 134–35: *Numerous lamps perform multiple tasks in the master bedroom.* PAGE 136: *An iconic SoHo streetscape.* PAGE 137: *The ottoman is made from antique carpet remnants that are as practical as they are handsome.*

This loft is definitely a guy's world, but we've made a few heartfelt nods to a softer side, including a curtained dressing room draped in a pretty print. The last time I went there, Andrew had propped up a portrait of himself as a young boy in that room. It could have gone anywhere, but I think he understood that this room is where it ought to be. He's very insightful that way, as I think all great parents usually are.

The children love being here on weekends. The sofas are so generously scaled and such workhorses that I knew both children and adults would spend a lot of time on them. Sometimes Andrew and his boys turn all the chairs in the living room to face the windows and settle in for the great New York City sport of people watching. When they do, that holiday spirit takes over and the room feels rather like a transatlantic cruise with lounge chairs facing the light or out to sea and the view.

For the walls, Andrew had a stash of nineteenth-century lithographs: hunting scenes and exotic safaris—just what you'd hoped for and expected. Because he'd always wanted to start collecting contemporary art, he asked me to help

him break out of that mold. Usually when someone asks me to do that, I say no, shying away because it's just too personal. This is one of the few times I've agreed to help on that level. As we hang the paintings, drawings, prints, and sketches that we're accumulating slowly, the apartment, too, has begun to evolve and embrace the personality of its residents. No longer empty, but rather full, this private club will always welcome new members.

Jeffrey Bilhuber **136** American Beauty

AMERICAN PASTORAL

A bundle of relations, a knot of roots, a family at home, planted among the oaks and apples

I glory in the American landscape, which is astonishingly handsome in its natural or transformed state. Where else but in this venerated bedroom community just north of New York City can you turn down a rutted dirt lane and happen upon a house so properly bucolic? There she sits, reassuringly balanced and symmetrical, amid old-growth beech, maple, and pine, backed up to Hook Road, that unpaved axle-breaker made memorable by a five-hundred-year-old *Quercus alba* at its corner—the Bedford Oak, a community treasure, majestic in its stateliness. Like that tree, David's life is planted deep in this Westchester haven, one of our country's earliest settlements, where the tracery of centuries-old bridle paths still connects neighbor to neighbor. His parents live with their menagerie of exotic animals but a mile away; another mile from there are his sister and her family. When he began his search for a house in the country, it was clear his destiny lay here. The

PRECEDING PAGES: *The stuccoed and limestone front facade of the English style cottage.* LEFT: *Lila's pink playhouse is tucked deep within the enchanted forest.* OPPOSITE: *The majestic Bedford Oak.* OVERLEAF: *A newborn camel frolics through the ancient apple orchard.*

140

handsome English-style cottage that he found needed a bit of attention, and then a bit more, its lovely proportions somewhat obscured.

The house presents itself quietly—but in a welcoming way—in a landscaped park deftly domesticated in the spirit of Capability Brown. Centuries-old dry-set stone walls meander through the property. Mature trees cast animated, shadow-dappled light. An orchard planted in a double crescent, decorative yet functional, bears fruit in the back garden. I've never seen an orchard in a double crescent—ever.

At our very first meeting, we all agreed that the visual goal for the interiors should be part Art Nouveau and a bigger part Arts and Crafts. This was a first. I'd never before explored such a creative directive, nor one expressed in such intellectual, even academic, terms. It offered me an opportunity to delve even more deeply into an area of decorative-arts history that I have always responded to for its romance and substance. The more I thought about what inspired us, the more I realized that it came down to the interpretation of nature and its organic forms. Art Nouveau traced the feminine strain, Arts and Crafts, the masculine. Their union proposed an inherently elegant way to weave together both perspectives, to express the essence of human interaction with the landscape, with the garden, with the botanic and handcrafted.

My vocabulary of ornament took on a florid romantic aura—so right for this family and house. This splendid interior landscape would inevitably involve a profusion of vines and leaves, flowers and fruit, disciplined by the roots and trunks that support them all. The daughter of the house, like all children, needed a place of her own, a brilliant pink castle of

sorts, for comfort and dreams. She selected it herself, including the color of course. When we become parents, the needs of our families infiltrate our environment. Welcome them we must, and do.

Not far from the castle is the cottage, entered through an intimate vestibule where a mirror reflects the whole of the landscape behind, a wondrous moment where the interior is transparent. The ground-floor rooms are in enfilade, with the paneled and painted living room the house's dignified tour de force—both living room and library, paired with bookcases on either end. I deliberately chose a hodgepodge of low-key furnishings, emphasizing charm over provenance—an English eighteenth-century gilded mirror with a ravishing patina, a pair of enchanting French provincial ladder-back chairs, lacy-but-solid 1910 wicker chairs. This very big room demanded a center table, and I found one of midcentury evolution with a painted iron base that owes much to Buckminster Fuller, a forgotten modern tinkerer—a sublime riff on the screening, lattice, filigree, and interlacing so intrinsic to the decor. The Moorish ottomans reiterate the allure of the exotic, a filtering of Art Nouveau's Orientalist strain.

LEFT: *Klover, a roller print from the first quarter of the twentieth century, papers the walls of the vestibule and bath.* OPPOSITE: *A marble-topped baker's table adds a lighthearted touch to the small entry hall.* OVERLEAF: *A view into the handsome paneled living room.*

guests there is an entire room of Maine cottage furniture, purchased the summer before on a visit to Nantucket because I knew it had to be. I love the naive pastoral imagery—so comforting and familiar—combined with a welcomed architectural flourish of scalloped festooning. I could happily sleep in that room forever. In the master bedroom, light filters playfully through handsomely proportioned windows—and once again through those intricate Syrian chairs, inlaid with the depth of ebony and reflection of abalone.

In retrospect, it seems that bringing this house back to its natural beauty had everything to do with its setting in nature and its occupants' love of family—that oblique approach to the house, the natural screens of the oaks and the pines, the fruits of that ancient orchard, the extraordinary light and shadow on a mature landscape, all right in their place, all offering tantalizing glimpses of what's to follow. When I imagine David and his family there, it's not the objects that I see nor those that I know we will continue to add to this place over time, but the joyful, well-lived lives the house embraces—the thwack of tennis balls in the background, children's laughter from the crenellated tower of the playhouse, picnics under a leafy canopy, books devoured in a favorite chair—and the memories being made just a right turn onto Hook Road.

A pomegranate dining room seemed predestined because of the house's Englishness. When the color went up, it was so spot-on that I knew there were no other options. The purple-based redness may seem a tinge stuffy, but I know it is right, as does David, who hesitated at first and delighted at last. It's the stuffiness of memory and appropriateness. David wanted a table that would accommodate meals and occasions large and small. I found a classic English triple-pedestal dining table that did just that, and I suggested it be scrubbed and bleached to look as if it were simply fading away. The Syrian chairs were among our first finds, and we later supplemented them with English and American wire furniture and nineteenth-century wicker, all of the same transparency and lightness.

In the private quarters, romance blooms. For

PRECEDING, LEFT: *A detail of the eighteenth-century English gilded mirror.* PRECEDING, RIGHT: *The purity of a white glazed Korean vessel shines in this book-lined room.* RIGHT: *A pair of Arts and Crafts wrought-iron sunflower andirons dresses the fireplace.*

OPPOSITE AND ABOVE: *Electrified painted tole sconces contain modern Edison bulbs.* OVERLEAF, LEFT: *The black wicker chairs are the same as those in the garden.* OVERLEAF, RIGHT: *A copper-topped pie safe used as a side table in the pool room vestibule has trellis-faced doors lined with copper screening.*

PRECEDING PAGES: *The dining room's commodious bay window projects into the garden and the orchard.* LEFT: *An African Crowned Crane, one of many in the family's menagerie.* OPPOSITE: *The pillows throughout are made of antique Indonesian batiks.*

PRECEDING PAGES: *In the master bedroom, a phalanx of Syrian chairs lines up along the window wall.* RIGHT: *A pair of sapphire glass bedside lamps illuminates a suite of Maine cottage furniture painted with pastoral scenes.*

RIGHT AND OPPOSITE: *Pink walls set off blue-and-green-painted cottage furniture, an enchanting bit of romance in the guest bedroom. These rooms will continue to evolve over the years, welcoming the layers of detail and history to follow.*

FAINTLY FAMILIAR
Like a friend from long ago

This couple has always signified the arrival of a new age. They were the very first people who found me because of something they had read on the Internet, which way back then was a very big deal. When I met them, I'm quite certain I hadn't constructed my web site. I doubt I'd ever heard the phrase, 'We saw it online.' Now, the Internet and my web site generate fifty percent of my work. Times have certainly changed.

Thinking back, the two of them were harbingers of a whole new society—the very smart, very talented, very eager young men and women who proceeded to revolutionize the way we communicate, the way we invest, and, really, the way we live. They hadn't collaborated with a decorator before—not surprising, given that they were in their very early thirties—so they were new to all of the possibilities and temptations. As we worked on their West Village loft, it took the path of modernity—perfectly reflecting them at that stage of their lives.

When their family started to grow, their interests did as well—a natural evolution for this couple, I think, because they've always had a keen appetite for new information and a real curiosity

PRECEDING PAGES: *The rooms in this house have the sensory perception of a great hotel in London, circa 1930; very plush and comforting.* LEFT: *A contemporary piece by Saul Sanchez enlivens the phantom closet door.*

168

about furniture and art. Planning for more children, they eventually moved to an apartment much farther uptown. Over several years, they slowly expanded that initial apartment into other neighboring ones until they had a lovely, classic, rambling Upper West Side family residence.

Then came the call: 'We've matured,' she said, 'and we need more wood.' In other words, 'We need more substance.' I took Erica quite literally, and the rooms became much better for it. People may state their preferences categorically, but later they balk at the new and retreat to the familiar. No struggles ensued here with the transition from downtown to uptown and from parchment to mahogany. Vestiges of that original apartment made the trip: vellum-clad bedside tables, lacquered Japanese trays, all of the upholstery, now newly recovered, the vast and graphic painting by Fonseca, and the woven metal screens (early twentieth-century New York City elevator doors). These objects fit in beautifully with the substantial English, Irish, and Scottish pieces we've assembled here—considerable purchases all, and a significant leap forward from where we started. The development of that mix feels organic and ongoing: there's the through-line of family, generation after generation of refining tastes and curiosities, evolving in discrete phases so natural in their development they are only recognizable in retrospect. Their collector's eye is astute and informed, and they continue to add art into their rooms.

A handsome pair of rather intimately scaled English *buffetieres* (you'll find their companion piece hugging the dining room wall) lends gravity to the living room, as does the very muscular Swedish bergère, with the most extraordinary carved wood and upholstered arms. The gilded French taboret adds a subtle burnished sparkle and flaking gesso into this world of polished wood. The marble top separates from the base, and you simply put it where you wish—in one room on Tuesday and another on Thursday, if you so desire. Her father, who had a more modernist vocabulary, gave them the incised and patinated bronze table by Philip and Kelvin LaVerne, a truly iconic mid-twentieth-century work—and especially lovely because it was a gift from her grandfather to her father and then from a father to his daughter.

I find anything ebonized alluring, because it patinates so well and is so very nuanced—as the

169

OPPOSITE: The Future, *an oil on canvas by Enrique Martinez Celeya, hangs above the tufted sofa covered in burnished silk.* ABOVE: *A pair of nineteenth-century Etruscan red-painted klismos chairs adds historical precedence to the mix of periods and styles in the living room.* OVERLEAF: *The Caio Fonseca painting moved with the owners from their first apartment. It reiterates the graphic movement of the Georgian crystal chandelier.*

dining room reveals. The nineteenth-century ebonized chairs around the English polished mahogany table are probably an Edwardian-Victorian hybrid, with a form, style, and finish that I love to this day. The design is clearly an English or Irish copy of a French shape: the silhouette obviously has its origins in the 1860s, but the reeding, the fluted legs, and the stretcher, though very refined details, are not original to those periods.

As the apartment continued to expand and accommodate the family's needs, we found ourselves rethinking the function of various rooms. The original dining room became the family room early on because of its proximity to the kitchen; the dining room was meant to be the library because it opened off the living room. When the family room moved to another part of the apartment after the

second expansionist phase, it became the library. A lot of the libraries I design are not really for lounging, but rather cataloging or reference: they facilitate the getting or storing of books, but reading takes place elsewhere. I really don't object to having books simply to look at or admire, though, in general, I have no interest in being in a room full of books when I'm reading just one.

The elevator entry hall presented a quandary that took some time to resolve. The reverse-painted glass was clearly the solution. Just to fit a room with glass is a meticulous operation. When you factor in the painting, it becomes an utterly consuming process: six months to cut the templates, do the handwork, and lay it in. Once inside the foyer, the apartment becomes that much more steadfast and peaceful—though I will confess that it wasn't until *You Are Here*, a seminal work by the artist Saul Sanchez appeared that the hall took on its full personality.

The master bedroom is part of the latest phase of the apartment, which is now everything they need it to be for the foreseeable future. I think this room provides an inkling of yet another phase in the making. It takes on a bit more of a 1930s personality, rather like a very deluxe suite at The Savoy or The Dorchester. With the glamorous, tufted Duchesse satin headboard and plush wool Wilton carpet underfoot, it's evidence of a lighter touch—a move past mahogany, perhaps, toward what may come next in the family's own ongoing evolution.

SUMMER FALLS
A thicket of a farm becomes a house in the village

I have found that people frequently search for a house in the country when they're not quite ready to commit to what they know must happen in town. More often than not, working on a charming cottage in a country setting provides a winningly attractive alternative to renovating a house in the city. City houses are just plain daunting. They are undertakings with millions of moving parts. This was certainly true for Jenny and Trey Laird, who happened upon this wonderfully mysterious property at a time when their children were young and they weren't yet ready to tackle major changes to their rather bohemian New York town house (see pp. 10–33). The front of the house presented itself as a cottage on a country lane, a cottage of 1920s vintage bearing some resemblance to a farmhouse, but a farmhouse as modified for town: set close to the street, with a porch opening onto a little driveway that traverses a little sidewalk stretching the entire lane from the village in one direction to the train station in the other, giving no indication of what lurked behind it.

Country lanes like theirs developed around the turn of the century for proximity to a new commuting society. To create a sense of neighborliness, they tended to feature very narrow, rather deep parcels of land, probably the first

PRECEDING PAGES: *Clouds of English boxwood border the garden path toward the one-car garage.*
LEFT: *A detail of the guest cottage bedroom.*

182

addition of a bathroom with a glamorous, if chaste, matte marble-slab shower. They continued to push further back, clearing the brush and identifying old-growth trees, until they finally, rather anticlimactically, reached the property's end.

Thanks to the glorious contributions of the esteemed landscape designer Deborah Nevins, the Lairds' property now contains a series of little 'green rooms,' which, rather like a village with a sidewalk, are linked by a path through that deep, narrow garden. Honestly, I think they have been a bit surprised that the house and garden they have created were what they were looking for all along. One walks from the house along that rather gracious gravel path toward a guesthouse, and farther along to an ancient butternut tree, the pool, and the pool house, and, finally, to a small paved spot built specifically for basketball or a rigorous game of Ping-Pong. This

subdivisions of much larger parcels of farmland. With houses pushed close to the street, the rest of the property behind most likely returned to its previous agricultural use, creating a community of suburban farms that single families could tend (or not)—an arrangement that accounts for the plain, diminutive sheds commonly set farther back on this type of property.

When the Lairds rounded the cottage to the back, what they discovered was a thicket of overgrown brush and trees, gone to seed and fallen into tangle. As they forged their way deeper through the brush, they were surprised by an evocative little two-room cottage, most likely meant to be a utilitarian workshop, which a previous owner had later domesticated with the

183

shaded path is bordered in boxwood and skirts the perimeter of the property—a decision that pushes the entire series of small structures out of focus, making you work to discover them, just as the Lairds had to on that very first day many years ago.

A pavilion style pool house—really two sentry boxes, one room each, connected by a loggia—is open on both sides like a breezeway. This airy, light-filled living room is at the property's deepest end and is where Jenny and Trey now spend most of their summer days and nights. They do everything there: swim laps, catch up on reading, nap under bowers of wisteria, host a swimsuit-and-barefoot lunch, challenge guests to try their best hoop shots, or do absolutely nothing at all. At the close of each day, they and their guests hike back to the main house, the original one, which now

serves as a series of intimate rooms and places to sleep, rather like The Sea Breeze Inn & Cottages.

The little guest cottage has the spirit of an artist's studio. It's only two rooms behind a hedge, where just the door is glimpsed: a little bedroom, and a pretty living room with a kitchen opening onto it. It is a very utilitarian place, with exposed shelves for stacking dishes and bowls. It's also marvelously easy to be in. That shower has never looked better, nor more tempting.

When Jenny and Trey travel, which is often, they visit cities and countries that strike their fancy. Wherever they go, they're always looking and discussing what they see, and they always will. They add their discoveries to their houses—a chair found in an antiques shop in Bridgehampton, a carpet found in Turkey, a hammered brass sculpture from Botswana. They love the process of it all and are happy for, and invigorated by, all of their finds, and the poetic still lifes they create from them.

They hold this house and its garden close to their hearts. Jenny has told me very clearly that whenever anyone asks how long they stay out there, she replies, 'to the bitter end.' I can see her there now, not a leaf on a tree, not a navigable path, the pool closed, the cottage too—just Jenny, aglow with the memories of the summer passed, dreaming of yet another.

LEFT: *The chairs in the guest room are provincial French, a forgotten form and finish worth revisiting.* OPPOSITE: *Enameled shades on the bedside lamps shield mercury bulbs.* OVERLEAF, LEFT: *The original marble slab shower was left intact.* OVERLEAF, RIGHT: *William's attic bedroom has all the trappings of a teenager's treehouse.*

PRECEDING PAGES: *Comfortable and durable, China matting is an appropriate material for the pool house floor.* LEFT AND OPPOSITE: *The pillows, all hand-blocked in India, are from John Robshaw, a great friend who has admirably taken these cottage crafts and made them a worthy industry.*

FOUR OAKS
At the mouth of the creek, history finds home

Called Four Oaks since the beginning of the twentieth century, this fieldstone house with its colonial-era foundations sits on what was once a 150-acre orchard deep in one of Pennsylvania's fertile, verdant, ore-and-limestone-rich valleys, whose Native American meaning translates to 'mouth of the creek.' Chartered in 1743 and settled by hardworking German immigrant farmers, this area was transformed into coal-and-steel country during the Industrial Revolution. Thanks to its natural mineral wealth and the rise of the railroads in the mid-nineteenth century, it became home to companies that evolved into Bethlehem Steel over the century and a half of that manufacturing powerhouse's

PRECEDING PAGES: *Olive-colored printed linen covers an arc-backed eighteenth-century Hepplewhite settee.* LEFT: *Lucky greets visitors at the front door.* BELOW: *A detail looking into the powder room.*

existence. In Bethlehem Steel's heyday, the company and its executives established their houses and families in this scenic farm country. Four Oaks is one of a series of eighteenth- and nineteenth-century Pennsylvania farmhouses that the company once owned and aggrandized in the 1920s or '30s for the use of its senior executives, along with other perks like membership in the area's best country club and, thus, a built-in social life.

Just how profoundly the history of this house and its land had influenced its current owners was apparent at our very first meeting: they arrived with several manila envelopes containing hundreds of photographs that documented their reclamation of the house. I was moved by the enormous pride they took in their labors and accomplishments. I was also

gratified that, after seeing my achievements on a mutual friend's house, they realized that there are many additional steps to take once the glories of structural restoration are complete. They were raising a proud, earnest, close-knit family in this house, having lived through the extensive restoration it required, and had recently started to replant the gardens. The time for the interior had arrived, a much-anticipated highlight for all.

LEFT: *The original eighteenth-century stairs remain intact.* ABOVE: *A recumbent stag in the entry.* OVERLEAF, LEFT: *The stenciled floor connects the entry and the living room.* OVERLEAF, RIGHT: *A crewel-work fabric covers a line-inlaid and cross-banded Sheraton armchair.*

201

PRECEDING PAGES: *Propped casually on a stack of books in the living room is a powerful oil on paper,* Study of Two Fishermen *by Albert Bierstadt, painted in 1857.* RIGHT: *Black-painted Maine wicker furniture fills the sun porch to overflowing.*

LEFT AND OPPOSITE: *The pretty, recolored toile on the headboard and curtains in the daughter's bedroom suits the room and its occupant. She has cleverly co-opted the curtain rod and used it for additional closet space.*

The house sits strong and sturdy in the landscape, with a field-paneled front door accentuated by the surprising flourish of two enchanting oval windows. The family Labrador, Lucky, usually watches over this entry, which was otherwise in want of a true sense of arrival. When I first saw the interiors, the walls were just too plain. What spoke volumes to me about where to begin was the family's dazzling collection of late nineteenth- to early twentieth-century American landscapes, from what I believe to be the New Hope School, a few of which are in their original period frames.

My cues for the entry hall came from Martha and George Washington's grand public receiving room at Mount Vernon, a room meant to enhance the regal trappings of its visiting dignitaries as well as the objects housed within. Entirely awash in Prussian blue, probably the eighteenth century's rarest, most magisterial dry pigment, the room framed the assemblage of carved and burnished export porcelains

and let the furniture glow. There are very few people who will instantly embrace the idea of a dark hall, so it was no surprise that this color took some persuading. Its historical accuracy was key to the conversation and the deciding factor in moving the blue hall forward. The depth and intentional application of this color establishes what I feel is a necessary separation between outside and inside, and it creates an interior that comforts in a rather noble way.

Like so many of its contemporaries, this house started with three or four narrow, smallish rooms set purposely in a row. Years of additions hadn't deviated from the original tight proportions, so to make the rooms feel inherently larger and to unify them into a coherent whole, I conceived a painted pattern on the floor of the entry and living room. The origins of that pattern are clearly European—and I make additional references to Europe in other aspects of the decoration here because we are a nomadic society—and I needed to reestablish the historical connection this house had to its geographic context. The Pennsylvania Dutch hex signs present in the surrounding farm country provided the visual touchstone I had hoped for—and a metaphor with a bit of irreverence.

One cardinal rule of design is that you cannot build a new old house. That's why you could never plan an internal window that occurs as gracefully as the one in this house. It clearly punctuates what was the terminal wall of the original house, and it tells us much about how the place has grown and evolved.

Linen hopsacking covers
the walls of the master
bedroom. The iron tester bed
is a contemporary find from
Hollyhock in Los Angeles.
I always favor bed hangings,
especially in historic houses.

210

A framed piece of broderie perse *hangs inside the canopy at the head of the bed. The enchanting paper tag at the base reads, 'Made about 1852 by Mary Cornelia Fitzgerald Monroe, grandmother of Mary Cornelia (Ninie) Monroe Covington, who had it framed in 1934.'*

LEFT AND OPPOSITE: *In the breakfast room, American beadwork flora and fauna add touches of whimsy and sparkle. A Charles II oak molded-front chest from the seventeenth century makes reference to the joinery and hardware found throughout Four Oaks.* OVERLEAF: *In the family room, a nineteenth-century English reading chair contributes to the atmosphere of relaxed comfort.*

The deeply set living room windows are purposely unadorned, as they should be. The sunroom was added, and it is a kindred spirit to the sleeping porches that I've loved and admired in so many great Southern houses, and to the screened-in porches that make late afternoons in Maine such a pleasure.

The toile in their daughter's bedroom stands as a great metaphor for the history of the house, reimagined and recolored. The *broderie perse* in the master bedroom—antique chintz that's been cut out and sewn down and affixed to a cloth panel— represents exactly the goals and directions the owners found so valuable when they were renovating, restoring, and decorating, a casual and clear metaphor on my behalf.

The furniture in the breakfast room is not limited strictly to American forms, nor should it be. The assembled pieces—the French balloon-back chairs, the English pewter-and-brass chandelier, the

American folk art—express our American wanderlust, the urge we have to bring home with us furniture and decorative objects that help recall where we've been, as people and as a nation. The same spirit holds true at some of America's greatest houses, including Beauport and Arlington House.

The family room, another addition dating to I know not when, is on another plane altogether. You step down into it, which ceremoniously separates it from the bulk of the main structure. It is the one part of the house that really could become anything that we wanted because it was so comparatively new and represented the cleanest slate. As a result, the room starts to take on more of a European influence.

The decoration of this house may be a bit grander than its origins, but I'm quite sure it would have evolved along these lines, or similar ones, had it continuity to its history and ongoing prosperity. History teaches us much, and we must listen. If we do, a few simple truths prevail. You cannot restore an historic house overnight, nor should you try. It is vitally important to work slowly when preserving the heritage of a house and garden. Four Oaks embodies these truths. As farmland continues to be lost to development at an astounding rate, this green valley still retains its beautiful woodlands, streams, and rolling hills. Clearly the community and, most important, this family, have taken care to preserve what remains.

AN EDUCATION IN HAPPINESS
Green hedges, gravel driveways, swings from trees, daily dreams

Upon this family's first visit to the unassuming painted shingle house that they eventually would own, their son, then three, bubbled up: 'This is a happy house!' His premonition became the premise for what this enchanting bungalow should be. It was set on a picturesque street with the allure of every country lane ever conjured—picket fences, porches, sidewalks leading to a church, and lovely neighbors who had lived on this very street long enough to watch their children grow up and move away. This house, as a family project, grew to mean something much more to them than just a place to make pretty: it became their very first 'real' house they would know together. Here they were, a very talented and creative couple—relatively new parents—venturing from their urban comfort zone to purchase their very first house near the beach.

Separately, and now as one, they had for years imagined the ideals of union and partnership, the specific place where father meets mother meets son meets home meets dreams of their future. That thought process is part of an inspired collaboration that is characteristically theirs, as is the rich, joyous emotion that distinguishes all of their efforts. That's why I think of this family as the house's artists in residence, the

PRECEDING PAGES: *A flurry of glorious paper lanterns over the kitchen table is strung up from red and white baker's twine.* LEFT: *The lampshades are made from antique saris.*

220

people who give it a certain creative spirit and chutzpah (a word I love).

Artfully bohemian, contagiously optimistic, spontaneous, and exotic, their rooms are full of bits and pieces they have found in antique shops, flea markets, souks and bazaars around the world and mementos from their past, all assembled in a festive atmosphere. Actually, 'festive' is putting it mildly: this incredible family wears their hearts on their sleeves, and their inner happiness radiates to us all. Swaying from the branches of a shade tree are lanterns made of Mexican tin. On the interior, Japanese paper lanterns from the early twentieth century, equally as appealing, repeat that spontaneity and spirit; there to catch the breeze and movement of the air, they bob and dance when the windows and doors open or close.

How very liberating it was to work on this house is confirmed in my decision to have all the brilliant, clear-eyed colors collide: glacial blue, volcanic red, and festive fuchsia bump into one another and also into magenta and vermilion. The parasols in the kitchen fall into the category of 'things that are just too wonderful to pass up, so you simply find a way to fit them in.' They were a harebrained idea of mine to give this high-ceilinged room a better sense of scale and intimacy. The owners just adore them. As do I.

Really great houses inform others about us through a series of discoveries that are our decorative

LEFT: *Near the living room's salon-style tufted sofa is a painting by the magical American artist Nancy Lorenz.* ABOVE: *Red schoolhouse chairs attend the very long zinc-topped garden table.*

221

choices. This family happened to have a glorious, personality-driven collection of furniture and objects, purchases made from mind and soul. With so many telling pieces, what I really wanted to do was to link them together: the continental painted and gessoed table, the exotic carved elephant, the baluster lamps that we had painted in great big carnival stripes. The owners' enthusiasm is what connects all these components. I simply added the vigorous colors and the decorative glue to hold all the pieces together.

While we were working on the house, the owners kept extricating furniture and art from some obscure warehouse of theirs, or the farthest side of their garage, or the depths of a cellar that seemed, like Mary Poppins's bag, to get larger and deeper every time I looked in. They still continue to do this. They find great joy in these discoveries, or rediscoveries, to be more precise. There's always something new and amusing on the breakfast room table when I arrive, accompanied by a little note

PRECEDING PAGES: *The kitchen opens directly onto masses of seating around a fireplace and table. The configuration is similar to that of a lovely country house, except this is a bungalow in the village of East Hampton.*
OPPOSITE: *The kitchen worktable is used to prep and cook daily meals. The triple-tier wire vegetable stand is a very practical and enchanting solution.*
ABOVE: *A treasured vintage carnival case with trick cards rests on a bookshelf.*

PRECEDING, LEFT: *A French farmhouse table with chamfered corners offers ease of access. All table linens are Mexican, vintage, and embroidered.* PRECEDING, RIGHT: *The vintage paper lanterns are too fragile to ever light again, but they will always animate the breakfast table.* LEFT: *Summer zinnias on the dining table repeat colors and patterns of the ancient paper lanterns in the kitchen.* OPPOSITE: *In the living room, exuberant colors and patterns mix with the owners' diverse collection of antiques.* OVERLEAF, LEFT AND RIGHT: *Upholstering the tufted ottoman is a quilted Indian bedspread.*

PRECEDING, LEFT: *A detail of an exuberant Mexican tin mirror.* PRECEDING, RIGHT: *Dahlias and impatiens are classic beachside summer flowers.* LEFT: *Patchwork pillows incorporate antique and vintage fabric fragments.* BELOW: *The French chairs have scrubbed oak frames.* OPPOSITE: *Garden and beach hats hang on the coatrack in the hall.* OVERLEAF, LEFT: *In the laundry, all-purpose zinc factory lights illuminate a farmhouse sink.* OVERLEAF, RIGHT: *Drying ladders brim with several of the owners' vintage table linens.*

For the guest bedroom, I had imagined a shimmering place to dream dreams, a bed that sparkles and shines. Neither she nor he paused when I conceived of beaded, curtained bed hangings. I do confess, it's a very fine place to be, and more than a bit inspired. They were right to love it, from its genesis to its whimsical realization.

There's a palpable romance in this house and an immediate emotional resonance. Mostly, there's the laughter that bubbled up from their son when they first saw it. I think of this house as a kind of year-round Valentine's Day gift filled with a sentiment that makes everyone who visits feel very much in love. The owners' belief in human kindness, in innate goodness, in putting others first, and their concern about this very fragile world that we live in—it is all expressed here, with a bit more sparkle, and pizzazz, and three very big hearts.

saying, 'Hope we can use this!' Or, 'Give this a shot!' Or, 'I love these, hope you do too!' These missives are poems shared with me about the objects they'd like me to work with, and love as much as they do.

The living room revolves around a Parisian salon–style sofa, which I made as big and red and tufted as possible. As for the pair of no-longer-matching chairs, one is in a brilliant cotton-candy pink, the other in clementine orange. They bookend the sofa in a way that forces you to look at them two or three times to confirm they are similar yet slightly different from each other. In a flash of inspiration, I realized that this room needed a more south-of-the-border sensibility—hence the exuberant, elaborate Mexican tin mirror, rendered with much finesse and detail. I covered the massive ottoman in a printed cotton bedspread that started as one of those fabled 'Hope we can use this, it's my favorite!' items. Armfuls of these fabrics would simply appear, and they soon became lampshades, chairs, pillows, and slipcovers.

RIGHT: *Two housekeepers create a beautiful, exotic bed inside the shimmering beaded curtains.* OVERLEAF, LEFT: *A late 1930s Italian, etched, blush glass mirror.* OVERLEAF, RIGHT: *A detail of the bed's interior glories in a festival of red and white patterns.*

LEFT: *A treasured memento is this amusing Venetian glass mermaid.* OPPOSITE: *One of a pair of painted French bistro chairs, snug by the bookcase.* OVERLEAF, LEFT: *The walls are stenciled with a classic Indian border pattern.* OVERLEAF, RIGHT: *An antique devotional painting presides over a tower of lacquered storage trunks.*

A HOUSE AT THE CROSSROADS
Traveling the world to turn home

There's something rather evocative about the Turtle Bay neighborhood in Manhattan. Just the whisper of the name conjures up specters of the city's creative Parnassians: Katharine Hepburn and Stephen Sondheim; Henry Luce and Garson Kanin; Leopold Stokowski and Maxwell Perkins; E. B. White, who wrote *Charlotte's Web* when he lived on Forty-eighth Street; the great jurist Learned Hand. Of course, there's the obvious as well: the United Nations, the true crossroads of the world. I lived in Turtle Bay, rather elegantly, for three years. It used to thrill me to see hundreds of people in their native dress when I walked from my front door.

Turtle Bay town houses have never been truly grand, but they have always had a real sense of neighborliness and community and—or at least so one feels—an embrace of a much wider world beyond their walls. Tami Goven and Paul Stoneham's house expresses some of that global connectivity. That may be because they have traveled this world with great ease and returned home with many mementos that now lend a certain weight to these intimate rooms. It may also be because soon after they settled

PRECEDING PAGES: *The parlor is a faithful recreation of the house's nineteenth-century original.* LEFT: *In the dining room, faceted mirrored reveals reflect Georgian crystal sconces.* OPPOSITE: *Carved wood sculptures of African hunts rest on a parlor table.*

into the house, they jumped the pond to take up residence in London, where they started again: not just any part of London, but glorious, enchanting Notting Hill, a part of London that's a bit like a global village. When I received a 'Change of Address' notice, soon followed by a birth announcement, it all seemed rather appropriate and poetic.

Now that they've returned to Turtle Bay, we've picked up just where we were. And yet none of us is the same. After three years of not visiting this house, for instance, I found myself responding to its intimacy in an entirely new way. Defined by its dimensions—a bit less than the standard twenty feet in width—it does not really welcome strictly formalized rooms, nor, at this point, do I. That's partly my evolution, but I now believe it's theirs as well.

With an entry hall just as wide as the two sets of double doors, the foyer simply draws you directly up the stairs. The moons of light I installed over the entry landing are a reference to the gas-driven globe fixtures that were once ubiquitous in houses such as this. When I affixed them, we felt we'd found the perfect, uncomplicated design—so very appropriate to the clarity and simplicity of the architecture, and softly luminous. The stairs, narrower than most, head ever higher toward the light, following these glorious moons on every floor.

When we worked on the house originally, we all agreed to move a number of Paul's touchstones from his bachelor days—a corner chair, a pedestal table with an inlaid top, an ivory inlaid chest, and a number of African and Canadian Inuit carvings among them—to a secondary position, since they did not translate very easily to the decorative language we were then developing. When I revisited recently, those very same pieces leapt to take a primary role:

that corner chair that had been sent down to the kitchen bounded upstairs with me very happily; the ebonized table from the family room slipped seamlessly into the living room. I think the family has come into its own, so clearly loving, growing, and evolving. The rooms had some remaining gaps that I've been filling in with this new perspective and insight. The Regency portraits in the living room add just a tiny touch of irreverence, a bit Edwardian, and a clear nod to that house they now call home abroad. Then there's the mirror over the mantel—the last piece of the puzzle, left unresolved for the past few years. When they knew they were coming back to New York, Tami asked me to find her something suitably glorious and exuberant (she's nothing if not enthusiastic!). I found just the ticket, a George II gilt wood mirror, mid-eighteenth century, which fits the

LEFT: *A stash of foul-weather gear is cloistered in the third-floor closet.*
OPPOSITE: *The restored entry doors and staircase remind me of a Hudson River lighthouse.*
OVERLEAF: *A few of the owners' extensive collection of antique suzanis blanket the parlor floor.*

PRECEDING, LEFT: *The Georgian mirror reflects powder horns and pomegranates.* PRECEDING, RIGHT: *Scattered throughout the living room is a set of charming Regency portraits.* LEFT: *Seventeenth-century Gobelin tapestry panels flank the chimney.* OPPOSITE: *A 1930s amber glass lamp illuminates an intimate seating arrangement.* OVERLEAF: *Mandarin oranges, scented geraniums, and old-fashioned parchment-colored carnations dress a massive single-plank trestle table.*

room seamlessly. It does not, however, stand five feet tall, as she had imagined. It's a mere twenty-one inches high, and it's perfection—a little squat and exactly the right proportion for what it needs to do, which is lower the elevation, not raise it.

I was reminded that I had installed four great mirrored reveals in the dining room because this house, like most, was darkest at its center, and needed not just light but full-on animation. The Georgian faceted-crystal sconces further enhance the effect. It's extremely difficult to find two, let alone four, matching sconces, and these, quite rare, materialized at the eleventh hour. I was also reassured to see one of my first forays into clear, bright color—specifically, apple green—because I knew the saturation of that brilliant hue would help banish the darkness at the house's core.

Tami took the bedroom as her enclave and domain. It's a lovely room that faces north, with filtered light washing in through three sets of French doors opening onto a series of Lilliputian balconies. She chose a color palette of garnet and amber. If you look closely, you'll see that I've used Fortuny fabrics here, beautifully burnished in gold, that help the light glisten as it glances off each chair and sofa.

The staircase runs from the base or foundation of the house to the top. A very utilitarian skylight, with no ornament at all, filters light down into the interior from above. When you're ascending the stairs, you feel as if you're walking up into the lantern of a lighthouse. The scullery floor, now the kitchen, acts as an anchor at the stair's lower terminus, just as it always had. These rooms are wide and low, and they give the Stonehams great comfort. As a point of comparison, I adore the weight of these lower rooms and just how naturally the rooms above them transfer a certain luminescence, a beacon to guide a family home, like a ship at sea approaching harbor. This is a house that has settled well, as have we all.

ABOVE: *Paul Stoneham's vast library of travel reference books packs a pair of bookcases in the study.* OPPOSITE: *Greek Orthodox icons glow on stenciled walls.* OVERLEAF: *A linen velvet sofa anchors the library. Nearby, an ebonized Edwardian armchair looks toward the garden.*

OPPOSITE: *A very ladylike painted bergère sits close to the canopied master bed.* RIGHT: *A salvaged compass from a forgotten ship nestles in a niche near the second floor landing.* OVERLEAF: *The staircase concludes in the kitchen, a former scullery.*

AFTERWORD
Finding Your Way

When I think about the rooms that have mattered most in my life, they are the ones that I've come to know and understand through experience, memory, or enlightenment. Their details lodge, immutable, in my mind, and I revisit them often.

Familiarity with a house involves all the senses. Part of knowing a place is the physical or the tangible; part is purely emotional, and invokes the spiritual aspect of home. Crossing a threshold, passing through a portal, leaving what's outside to enter inside, engenders certain feelings and emotions in each of us that can vary according to the where, why, when, how, and with whom. The caress of a well-laundered sheet and its particular scent tends to stay with us over time. The discovery of a charming, intimate painting that somehow previously escaped our attention creates a lovely sense of surprise, and helps us anticipate other discoveries to follow. Although memory records our perceptions, the accuracy of these recollections is subject to interpretation because, of course, memory is not perfect. Even so, we can recall the nuances of experiences past—what they were, tangibly, and the way they made us feel. For instance, our ability to recall images or scenes allows us to revisit the way light washes through a specific room at a precise time of day, flooding our senses and making us aware of all the objects set

before us. That kind of memory is contained, complete, and comforting.

Enlightenment is something else altogether, an admirable and singularly human virtue that compels us to pursue knowledge, education, and research through reading, observation, and participation. These efforts remind us of our personal history as well, which we often document through our family lives. When I use the word family, I mean it in the broadest sense: our community and neighbors; our friends and those whom we deeply love; our forefathers, elders, and parents; or closer to home, our wives, husbands, and children. Considering the generational increments of familial relationships helps me understand my own memories. The associations I have with the objects that surround me help illustrate my life, and that of my son, Johann Christoph.

In the nearly four and a half years since his birth, I have revisited much of what I consider to be the basic truths of domestic bliss. This is not unusual, as we intuitively catalogue our memories and place them in a hierarchy. Our lives evolve as our culture shifts, and our needs change. As change presses against the glass of our windows, we regularly revisit the question of what kind of house we want most to return home to. Increasingly, this involves retreating to the comfort of the familiar.

Johann Christoph gets his name from his early eighteenth-century ancestor, the very first Johann Christoph (1702–1762). As my son grows older, I want him to understand where he comes from— why he is who he is, and who he just might be. This does not matter to him now, nor will it in the near future. It will take hold, as it did for me, somewhat on the sunset side of middle age. It was only at that point that I began to understand what a blessing it is to have one's family mementos close. These objects have real stories that very often contribute to the larger narratives of our lives.

I wonder what Christoph will remember from his early years, from our apartment in the city and our house in the country. As we look forward to our future, we must reflect upon our past. Recently, as I began to share my memories of home with my family, my parents, siblings, and close relatives started searching for certain mementos that I remembered from my childhood. Tangible objects began to emerge from attics, cellars, linen closets, chests of drawers, and safe deposit boxes. Many of them have materialized since Christoph's birth, appearing as gifts under a Christmas tree, birthday presents, or on a weekend visit with my mom and dad. The tenderness these objects has elicited, and the comfort they give me, has nourished all of us. I can only wonder if they will provide the same security and strength to my son. What was once my ancestors' is now intertwined with our own lives and helping build new narratives.

My two or three dozen mementos are a fraction of what my parents had from their parents, and an even smaller increment of what their parents had from theirs. Over the years many others have gone to my brothers and their families, whose own deep connections to and recollections of these objects now connect us all to our families.

The houses in this book represent versions of what home means to those who live there, and in many ways, to me, and in some others, to all of us. The way home is an evolutionary process. These pages offer a deeply personal, intimate view of how these homeowners 'tend their gardens.' Their houses, apartments, and cottages are the kinds of homes we want to go to, physically, emotionally, and spiritually. I do not expect any of the people in this book to keep their houses just as they are presented here, or to retain all the objects that are in them now. Yet I do believe that however many changes they might make to these rooms in years to come, they will long remember how happy these places and objects have made them feel. If home is just a metaphor for here, it's the here full of comforts, the here where we are happiest, and the place we are most at home with ourselves and those whom we love.

Welcome home.

DEDICATION

Written in these pages
A record going back into the Ages
Of our family, father and son
And the life-span of each one
Through several hundred years.
In every line may be found
Characters strong and sound
Who, departing, left behind them
Courage and determination
To each succeeding generation.
Even thus may we
Transplanted to a virgin shore
Follow this tradition as of yore
To let today's joy and sorrow
Help us hold together for tomorrow
And pledge our heart and hand
That united we may stand
Evermore!

Dedication verse by Ernst August Bilhuber
from *The Story of the Bilhuber Family,*
Summer 1909

ACKNOWLEDGMENTS

'American Beauty' found 'The Way Home' with the arrival of William (Bill) Abranowicz, the brilliant, acclaimed photographer who listened to my ideas and inspirations at our first meeting, and exceeded my expectations with the images he delivered. Pictures that will last a lifetime or two—perhaps more. It was after he submitted the first four chapters that I realized the narrative of the images told a slightly different tale than the one we had set out to capture. The pictures spoke of a way home that is a part of all of us, regardless of our backgrounds or origins, and reflects the dignity of all people, embracing our common humanity, and confirming not so much their circumstances but the truth about the people who live there. I am honored to have worked with him and his astute assistant, Christian Harder, as they both intuitively embraced the atmosphere and noble humanitism of this book.

Doug Turshen is considered a wizard in the field of art direction, and he brought, with his earnest assistant Steve Turner, their considerable talents to the development of these chapters. As the images helped me verbalize what only I had been able to visualize, the tenor of the book continued to evolve. For that I am grateful to Judith Nasatir, who helped cobble together my words in a way that made me hear more accurately what I had been speaking of so passionately these past few years. An orchestra is only as good as its conductor and I'm grateful to my editor, Isabel Venero, for her ability to combine the strings, the winds, and the percussion of this score.

Selecting projects that fit the American point of view in this book was an arduous task as I am honestly committed to all the efforts my office has helped me accomplish these past few years. Editing to fit the narrative was a difficult task made much easier by everyone in my design studio, and the generosity of my clients, who allowed me to share their stories. It speaks volumes that I selected twelve houses to tell twelve stories and made twelve phone calls to request their consideration for inclusion. Every request was greeted with pleasure and generosity, and each welcomed us back into their lives with admiration and into their homes with hospitality.

If it is true that we are defined by those we choose to surround us, then I am in good company. For that I am truly grateful.

First published in the United States in 2011 by
Rizzoli International Publications, Inc.
300 Park Avenue South
New York, NY 10010
www.rizzoliusa.com

Copyright © 2011 Jeffrey Bilhuber
Photography copyright © 2011 William Abranowicz

"East of The Sun (West of the Moon)" lyrics copyright
© 2011 the Trustees of the Princeton University Triangle
Club; used by permission.

2011 2012 2013 2014 / 10 9 8 7 6 5 4 3 2 1

ISBN 13: 978-0-8478-3573-7
Library of Congress Control Number: 2011927162

Designed by Doug Turshen with Steve Turner

Printed in China